FAVOURITE CHRISTMAS RECIPES

*Traditional
seasonal fare*

with illustrations by
Charles T. Howard

D0333056

Index

Copyright, Printed and Published by J. Salmon Ltd., Sevenoaks, England ©

Pork and Chestnut Pie

Light and tasty, this pie combines the traditional flavours of Christmas.

12 oz. flour   4 oz. butter   2 oz. lard
½ teaspoon salt   3 fl.oz. water
FILLING
12 oz. pork fillet, chopped roughly
12 oz. tinned whole chestnuts, chopped roughly
12 oz. cranberries   1 small onion, finely chopped
1 tablespoon cooking oil   1 teaspoon chopped thyme
1 teaspoon chopped sage   3 eggs, beaten   Salt and pepper

In a bowl, rub the fats into the flour and stir in the salt. Mix to a dough with the cold water, wrap in cling film and chill for 1 hour. Set oven to 400°F or Mark 6. Heat the oil in a pan and cook the onions until soft but not browned. Place the pork and chestnuts in a large bowl and add the onion. Stir in the herbs and seasoning to taste and mix well. Beat 2 eggs and add to the bowl with the cranberries, stirring thoroughly to combine. Roll out two thirds of the pastry on a floured surface and line a loose based 9½ inch flan tin. Fill with the pork mixture, smoothing it out evenly. Roll out the rest of the pastry to make a lid, cover and seal the edges with water. Beat the remaining egg and brush over the pie to glaze. Bake for 40-50 minutes. Serve hot or cold.

Christmas Goose

Goose is reputed to have the finest flavour of all domesticated birds. The reason for this is probably due to the high amount of fat it contains which gives the bird a very rich flavour. Save the fat in the roasting tin for the best ever roast potatoes.

1 ovenready goose 9-10lb
STUFFING

2 oz. butter	**4 fresh sage leaves, finely chopped**
1 large onion, finely chopped	**1 teaspoon salt**
6 oz. fresh white breadcrumbs	**Pepper**

Set oven to 425°F or Mark 7. Melt the butter in a saucepan and add the onion. Cook gently until soft, but not browned. Mix the butter and onion with the breadcrumbs, sage leaves and salt and pepper. Stuff the goose with this mixture and place on a rack in a large roasting tin. Prick the bird all over with a skewer to allow the fat to escape during cooking. Rub a little salt and pepper into the skin and place the tin just below the middle of the oven and roast for 20 minutes. Cover the breast with greased foil and reduce the heat to 325°F or Mark 3 and cook for about 3½-4 hours or until the juices run clear when a skewer is pushed into the thickest part of the leg, close to the body. To make the skin really crisp, remove the foil for the last 20 minutes of cooking time. Leave to rest for 15 minutes before carving.

Apple and Prune Stuffing

Apples have been a popular accompaniment to roast goose for centuries and in this traditional Christmas stuffing they are married with prunes. Apple and Prune Stuffing can also be served with duck or with roast pork.

12 large prunes
1 oz. butter
1 onion, finely chopped
2 cooking apples, peeled, cored and chopped
1 stick celery, finely chopped
1 oz. cooked rice (optional)

1 level dessertspoon finely chopped parsley
¼ teaspoon finely chopped rosemary
Pinch of ground mace
Rind and juice of half a lemon
1 to 2 teaspoons brown sugar
Salt and black pepper
A little beaten egg to bind

Soak the prunes overnight, if necessary. Next morning, remove the stones and chop roughly. Melt the butter in a saucepan and cook the onion until soft, then stir in the apple and celery and cook, stirring, for 2 minutes. Stir in the cooked rice, if used. Mix the herbs and mace together in a basin, then add the prunes, apple mixture, lemon rind and juice and brown sugar. Season, bind with a little beaten egg and spoon into the cavity of the goose. Some cooks like to add the goose liver to the stuffing. If this appeals, the liver should be fried in a little butter, chopped finely and added to the stuffing with the cooked rice.

Mushroom Sauce

This was a popular 19th century sauce and a traditional accompaniment to roast goose when served at Christmas or Michaelmas. Mushroom Sauce is also good served with roast pork.

1½ oz. butter
1 small onion, finely chopped
4 oz. mushrooms, finely chopped
1 oz. flour

¼ teaspoon dry mustard
¾ pt. rich brown stock or chicken stock
Salt and pepper
1 tablespoon port or white wine

Juice of half a large lemon

Melt the butter in a saucepan, add the onion and cook until soft and just golden. Stir in the mushrooms. Mix the flour and mustard together, add to the vegetables and cook for 1 minute, stirring. Gradually add the stock, stirring all the time. Bring to the boil and simmer for 5 minutes. Season, add the port or white wine and the lemon juice, then heat through thoroughly. Pour into a warmed sauceboat and serve with the roast goose.

Honey-roasted Turkey

First introduced into Britain in the 16th century, it was in the Victorian period that roast turkey really came into its own as a main Christmas course. The butter/honey mixture gives the meat a delicious flavour and adds a rich, dark crust to the skin.

1 oven ready turkey, 8 to 10 lb.	Salt and black pepper
1 small apple, peeled	A thick slice of lemon
1 small onion, peeled	3 oz. butter
1 small potato, peeled	6 oz. thick honey

Place inside the turkey the apple, onion and potato (they will help to keep the turkey meat moist) and season lightly. Place the turkey in a roasting tin and rub the skin lightly with the lemon. Melt the butter and honey together, stirring, and pour the mixture over the turkey. Allow to stand for about 30 to 40 minutes, spooning over the butter/honey mixture frequently. Set oven to 400°F or Mark 6. Allow approximately 15 minutes per pound of turkey. Roast for 30 minutes, basting from time to time. Reduce oven to 350°F or Mark 4 and roast for a further 30 minutes, basting from time to time. Cover with foil and continue cooking until the juices run clear when a skewer is pushed into the thickest part of the leg, close to the body. For the last 15 minutes of cooking remove the foil to crisp the skin. Leave to rest for 15 minutes before carving.

Chestnut and Bacon Stuffing

Chestnut stuffings were popular in the 18th century. A large bird such as a turkey is stuffed to prevent the meat from drying out too much during the long cooking time. This recipe will stuff a 10-12 lb. turkey.

1 oz. butter
1 large onion, finely chopped
4 oz. streaky bacon, diced
1 lb. tinned whole chestnuts,
    finely chopped

4 tablespoons chopped fresh parsley
1 dessertspoon chopped fresh thyme
Pinch of ground mace
8 oz. pork sausage meat
1 egg, beaten

Salt and pepper

Heat the butter in a frying pan and add the onion and bacon. Cook for 10 minutes, then remove from the heat and mix in a bowl with the remaining ingredients. Leave covered in a cool, but not cold, place until ready to stuff the turkey. The stuffing must be cold, but not icy cold, when it goes into the bird.

Celery Sauce

Celery, served as a vegetable or a sauce, is a traditional accompaniment to roast turkey, the flavours complementing each other perfectly.

1 small head of celery, finely chopped
1 small onion, finely chopped
2 oz. butter
1 oz. flour
Pinch of dry mustard powder
¾ pt. turkey or chicken stock

4 sprigs parsley, 1 spring of thyme and a
   small bayleaf, tied together with string
Salt and black pepper
Pinch of ground nutmeg
2 egg yolks
¼ pt. double cream

Mix together the onion and celery. Melt the butter in a saucepan and add the vegetables and cook until soft but not brown. Mix the flour and mustard powder together, then stir in to the vegetables and cook, stirring, for 1 minute. Gradually pour in the stock, stirring all the time, then add the herbs and bring to the boil. Simmer for 10 to 15 minutes. Remove the herbs and season. Just before serving, combine the egg yolks with the cream, stir into the sauce with the nutmeg and heat through thoroughly, but do not allow to boil or it will curdle. Pour into a warmed sauceboat and serve with the roast turkey.

Venison and Chestnut Casserole

A rich, gamy casserole which is cooked slowly for a long time and needs to be started the night before.

3 lbs. venison, cubed	1 sprig thyme
1 pt. stout	1 small onion, finely chopped
¼ pt. red wine	3 tablespoons cooking oil
1 bay leaf	1 tablespoon flour
1 teaspoon juniper berries, crushed	Salt and pepper
	12 oz. tinned whole chestnuts

Place the venison, stout, wine and herbs in a bowl, cover and leave overnight. Next day, set oven to 275°F or Mark 1. Remove the meat from the marinade and drain well on kitchen paper, reserving the marinade. Heat the oil in a flameproof casserole and add the meat, a few pieces at a time, to brown them. Remove the meat from the pan and add the onion to the pan. Cook for a few minutes until lightly browned. Return the meat to the pan and stir in the flour. Gradually add the marinade and herbs, stirring all the time. Season to taste with salt and pepper. When the mixture reaches boiling point, cover and place in the oven and cook for 2-3 hours until the meat is tender. Add the chestnuts for the last 10-15 minutes of cooking time, until heated through.

Marmalade Glazed Ham

A home baked ham has a much better flavour than the shop bought ready cooked version. It is ideal for a buffet or Boxing Day tea. Some joints do not need soaking; check with the supplier first.

6-8 lbs. gammon joint, on the bone
2 tablespoons Seville orange
marmalade

Finely grated rind and juice
of 2 oranges
2 tablespoons Dijon mustard

Soak the joint overnight (if necessary) in cold water. Next day, set oven to 325°F or Mark 3. Place the joint in a large roasting bag or seal loosely in foil and put, skin side up, in a large roasting tin. Roast the gammon for 20 minutes per pound. Twenty minutes before the end of the cooking time remove from the oven and increase the heat to 425°F or Mark 7. Mix the marmalade with the orange rind and juice. Cut open the roasting bag or open the foil and, with a sharp knife, remove the rind from the joint, leaving the fat. Slash the fat diagonally into 'diamond shapes' and spread first with the mustard, then the marmalade, including the marmalade rind or chunks. Return to the oven for about 20 minutes until glazed. Serve hot or cold. If serving hot, let the joint stand for 15 minutes before slicing.

Spiced Prunes

These are an excellent accompaniment to baked ham and hot or cold goose.

1 lb. large prunes	2 bay leaves
2 pts. cold fresh tea	1 cinnamon stick
¾ pt. wine vinegar	6 juniper berries
8 oz. muscovado sugar	Rind of 1 lemon

Soak the prunes overnight in the cold tea. Next day, place the prunes in a saucepan with *half* the soaking liquor and bring to the boil. Cover and simmer gently for 10-15 minutes until just tender. Drain the prunes, reserving the liquid. Put the vinegar, sugar, herbs, spices and lemon rind in a pan and heat gently until the sugar is dissolved. Bring to the boil and boil rapidly for 5 minutes. Add ½ pint of the reserved liquid from the prunes and bring back to the boil. Pack the cold prunes into sterilised jars and pour over the liquid to cover. Cover immediately with tight fitting lids and keep until needed. These prunes may be eaten 24 hours after potting.

Spiced Beef

Eaten hot or cold, Spiced Beef is traditionally served on Christmas Day or Boxing Day, decorated with holly.

4 lb. rolled salted silverside
1 onion, sliced
1 small turnip, sliced
3 carrots, sliced
1 bayleaf
Water, stout or brown ale

12 cloves
2 oz. soft brown sugar
Juice of 1 lemon
½ teaspoon each ground cinnamon, allspice and nutmeg
1 level teaspoon mustard powder

Soak the meat in cold water overnight. Next day, rinse well and tie up with kitchen string to form a firm, neat joint. Put the onion, turnip and carrots in a large saucepan, place the meat on top, add the bayleaf then cover with cold water or a mixture of water and stout or brown ale. Bring to the boil, skim, then cover and simmer gently for 3½ to 4 hours. Leave to cool completely in the liquid. Set oven to 350°F or Mark 4. Drain the meat very well, place in a roasting tin and stick with the cloves. Mix together all the remaining ingredients and spread over the meat. Bake for 40 minutes, basting from time to time. Remove the string and serve hot or cold. Serves 4 to 6.

Plum Pudding

Most families have their favourite recipe for Christmas Pudding. Banned by the 17th century Puritans as being "unfit for God-fearing people", it became popular once again due to George I so enjoying the Plum Pudding which was served at his first Christmas dinner in England. Later, the Victorians developed it into the familiar, even richer Dickensian 'cannonball'.

4 oz. self raising flour	½ teaspoon mixed spice
4 oz. currants	½ teaspoon ground cinnamon
4 oz. raisins	½ teaspoon grated nutmeg
4 oz. breadcrumbs	2 eggs
4 oz. dark brown sugar	Juice and rind of a lemon
4 oz. shredded suet	4 tablespoons dark rum
1 large apple, peeled, cored and chopped	1 cup milk

Grease a 2 pint pudding basin. Mix all the dry ingredients together in a large bowl. Add the eggs, lemon juice and rind and rum and sufficient milk and stir well to produce a dropping consistency. Put the mixture into the basin. Cover and seal with greaseproof paper and kitchen foil and steam for 3 hours, topping up with boiling water as necessary. If the pudding is to be kept for a while before eating, steam for a further 3 hours before using. Serve with Hard Sauce. Serves 6.

Hot Spiced Cream

A delectable, spicy creamy sauce to accompany the Christmas pudding.

1 pt. double cream	4 teaspoons ground cinnamon
4 teaspoons ground ginger	4 tablespoons light, soft brown sugar

Put all the ingredients into a non-stick pan and heat gently, stirring, until the sugar has dissolved. Bring to the boil, then reduce the heat and simmer gently for 2-3 minutes before serving.

Hard Sauce

Also known as Brandy Butter, this is a traditional accompaniment to Christmas Pudding.

4 oz. butter   4 oz. sugar   1 tablespoon brandy
2 tablespoons ground almonds or 1 drop of almond essence

Cream the butter and sugar together in a bowl and then gradually beat in the brandy and the ground almonds. Put into a serving dish and refrigerate until required. Serve with any kind of steamed plum or fruit pudding.

Iced Christmas Pudding

*A cold and creamy alternative for those who find the rich, traditional
Christmas pudding too heavy after Christmas turkey or goose.*

4 oz. mixed dried fruits:	**1 cinnamon stick**
raisins, currants, sultanas	**3 eggs**
2 oz. glacé cherries, chopped	**4 oz. sugar**
4 tablespoons rum or brandy	**¾ pt. whipping cream**
16 fl. oz. creamy milk	**1 oz. toasted almonds, chopped**

Soak the dried fruits and cherries in the rum or brandy overnight. Next day, pour
the milk into a pan and add the cinnamon stick. Heat gently until just about to boil,
then remove from the heat, cover and leave for 30 minutes. Remove the cinnamon
stick and reheat the milk over a low heat. Whisk the eggs and sugar together in a
bowl then pour on the hot milk, whisking all the time. Return the mixture to the pan
and heat, stirring, until the custard has thickened, but do not allow to boil. Remove
from the heat and leave to cool, stirring from time to time. Whip the cream until
thick but not stiff and fold into the custard with the fruits, soaking liquor and
almonds. Pour into a pudding basin then cover and freeze until firm. Place in the
refrigerator for 30 minutes before turning the pudding out on to a serving plate.
Decorate with a sprig of holly just before serving.

Light Christmas Pudding

A tasty, sponge pudding made with candied fruits, which is a lighter alternative to the traditional, dark rich pudding.

4 oz. glacé cherries, sliced thinly	3 oz. fresh white breadcrumbs
2 oz. candied peel, sliced thinly	Grated rind 1 lemon
3 oz. glacé pineapple, sliced thinly	6 oz. butter
1 oz. angelica, sliced thinly	6 oz. light soft brown sugar
2 oz. flaked almonds	3 eggs
3 oz. ground almonds	6 oz. self raising flour

Slice the candied fruits thinly and use some to arrange, attractively, over the base and sides of a well buttered 2 pint pudding basin. Put the remaining fruits, flaked almonds, ground almonds, breadcrumbs and lemon rind into a mixing bowl and stir well together. In another bowl, cream the butter and sugar until light, then beat in the eggs, adding a little flour to prevent curdling and beat well. Sift in the flour and fold in with a metal spoon. Gently fold in the fruit mixture until well mixed. Spoon carefully into the pudding basin and level the top. Cover with greaseproof paper pleated to allow for expansion, then cover with foil, also pleated, and seal well. Steam for 2½ hours, topping up with water as necessary. Remove the foil when cooked, cool in the basin for 15 minutes, and turn out. Serve with custard or cream.

Rum Butter Tarts

These delicious spicy fruit tarts make a change from the usual mince pies.

8 oz. rich shortcrust pastry	2 oz. dark soft brown sugar
2-3 oz. 'no soak' dried apricots, finely chopped	1 egg, beaten
2 oz. raisins	1 oz. ground almonds
1 tablespoon dark rum	½ teaspoon ground cinnamon
2 oz. butter	Pinch grated nutmeg
	Pinch ground cloves

Set oven to 375°F or Mark 5. Mix the apricots and raisins with the rum and leave to stand for about 15 minutes. Meanwhile roll out the pastry thinly on a floured surface and cut into 12-15 rounds with a pastry cutter. Line 3 inch greased patty or bun tins with the pastry rounds. Cream the butter and sugar in a bowl until light and fluffy, then beat in the egg, ground almonds and spices. Stir in the rum-soaked fruit. Place a spoonful of filling in each pastry case and bake for 15-20 minutes. Cool the tarts in the tins for a few minutes before transferring to a wire rack until cold. Serve warm or cold dusted with a little icing sugar.

Old English Nog Tart

The traditional ingredients of cream, alcohol and nutmeg produce a rich custard tart.

6 oz. flour   4 oz butter   ½ pt. creamy milk
3 tablespoons ground almonds   6 tablespoons caster sugar
¼ teaspoon grated nutmeg   2 eggs, separated   3 teaspoons powdered gelatine
3 tablespoons dark rum   6 tablespoons double cream   Grated nutmeg to finish

Set oven to 400°F or Mark 6. Rub the butter into the flour and stir in the ground almonds and 3 tablespoons of the caster sugar. Add a little of the milk and mix to a soft dough. Roll out on a floured surface and use to line a deep, loose based 8 inch flan tin or cake tin. Bake blind for 10-15 minutes, then leave to cool. Heat the remaining milk with the nutmeg. Beat the 2 egg yolks and 1 egg white with the rest of the caster sugar, then pour on the hot, but not boiling milk. Return the mixture to the pan and heat, stirring, until thick, but do not allow to boil or the mixture will curdle. Remove from the heat and cool slightly. Sprinkle the gelatine over the rum in a small cup and when it sponges (about 5 minutes) stir into the hot custard, stirring well. Leave to stand until beginning to set. Whip the cream until thick but not stiff. Whisk the remaining egg white until stiff. Gently fold the cream into the custard, followed by the egg white. Place the mixture in the baked flan case, chill until set, and then sprinkle with grated nutmeg.

Christmas Syllabub

Originally, syllabub was a festive drink made from fresh milk and wine, ale or cider, which gradually evolved into a dessert. It became very popular at parties in the 18th century.

Pared rind and juice of 1 small lemon	**2 oz. raisins**
6 tablespoons sweet white wine	**2-3 oz. icing sugar**
1 tablespoon medium sweet sherry	**½ pt. double cream**
2 tablespoons brandy	**Grated nutmeg to finish (optional)**

Put the thinly pared lemon rind and the juice, the wine, sherry, brandy and sugar into a bowl with the raisins and leave to soak for at least 3 hours or overnight. When ready, remove the lemon rind. Add the cream and whisk until the mixture stands in soft peaks. Pile into serving glasses and chill before serving. Just before serving, dust the top with finely grated nutmeg (if liked).

Christmas Compote

All the flavours of Christmas are present in this delicious fruit compote. It can be prepared well ahead of time and stored in the refrigerator.

1 pt. red wine
6 oz. soft brown sugar
2 sticks cinnamon
6 cardamom pods, bruised
  (optional)
A thick strip of orange zest
Juice of 1 orange

4 oz. kumquats, halved and pips
  removed
2 oz. cranberries
4 oz. 'no-soak' dried apricots
4 oz. 'no-soak' dried prunes
4 oz. raisins
2 oz. dried figs, halved

Put the wine, sugar, spices, orange zest and juice with the kumquats into a saucepan and heat gently until the sugar has dissolved. Bring to the boil and simmer for 10-15 minutes. Add all the dried fruit and simmer for about 15 - 20 minutes or until just softened to personal taste. Then add the cranberries and simmer for about a further 4 minutes until the cranberries are soft but still whole. Transfer all the fruit to the serving bowl with a slotted spoon, at the same time removing the cinnamon stick and orange zest. Bring the wine mixture back to the boil and boil rapidly until reduced by about half. Pour over the fruits, cool, cover and chill in the refrigerator for several hours before serving. Serve with whipped cream, crème fraîche or ice cream, as preferred.

Christmas Trifle

A proper trifle should be a sumptuous concoction of cake, creamy custard, alcohol and fresh cream. Custard powder or a top quality, ready made fresh custard can be used to save time, if preferred.

12 sponge fingers	4 oz. raspberries
Raspberry jam	1 pt. custard
4 oz. ratafia biscuits, crumbled	¾ pt. double cream
4 tablespoons sweet sherry	1 oz. icing sugar
3 tablespoons orange liqueur (optional)	Crystallised rose petals, flaked almonds and raspberries to decorate

Spread the sponge fingers liberally with jam, then break them up and place in a glass or china serving dish with the crumbled ratafias. Mix the sherry with the liqueur (if using) and pour over the sponge fingers and ratafias, mixing very gently and leave until the sherry is absorbed. Scatter the raspberries over, then spoon the cooled custard on top. Cover with cling film and chill in the refrigerator. Finally, whip the cream and icing sugar until soft peaks form and spread on top of the custard. Decorate with crystallised rose petals, flaked almonds and raspberries just before serving.

Chocolate Rum Truffles

These delectable 'melt-in-the-mouth' morsels are traditionally eaten at Christmas.
They are delicious with the after dinner coffee.

6 oz. plain chocolate	**2 tablespoons dark rum**
4 fl. oz. double cream	**Cocoa powder or icing sugar for dusting**

Break the chocolate into small pieces. Heat the cream in a saucepan and bring slowly to the boil. Remove from the heat and add the chocolate, stirring until melted. Add the rum and leave the mixture to cool for 30 minutes. Whisk the mixture until it holds its shape, then chill until firm enough to handle. Dust the hands with icing sugar or cocoa powder and shape the mixture into small balls. Roll in icing sugar or cocoa powder and chill. The truffles can be kept in an airtight tin in a refrigerator for up to 3 days.

White Christmas Candy

Delicious with coffee at the end of a meal. The ingredients are measured in cups; use a ¼ pint cup or a measuring jug.

2½ cups Rice Crispies   **1 cup full cream milk powder**
1 cup desiccated coconut   **½ cup mixed dried fruit**
¾ cup icing sugar   **½ cup glacé cherries, chopped**
8 oz. solid white vegetable fat or butter

Mix all the dry ingredients in a large mixing bowl, then stir in the fruits. Heat the vegetable fat or butter until melted but not hot and add to the bowl, mixing well to combine. Press the mixture into a 8 inch x 12 inch baking tin lined with non-stick baking paper. Chill overnight in the refrigerator. Cut into squares or festive shapes.

Port Wine Jelly

*Cool and refreshing after a heavy meal, this jelly is an alcoholic treat,
but not for children!*

1 oz. powdered gelatine	**1 stick cinnamon**
3 fl. oz. cold water	**Grated rind and juice**
6 oz. caster sugar	**of 1 lemon**
4 cloves	**½ pt. water**
Blade of mace	**½ pt. port wine**

Sprinkle the gelatine over the 3 fl.oz. cold water in a small bowl or cup. When spongy, after about 5 minutes, stand the bowl in hot (not boiling) water until the gelatine has melted and the mixture is clear. Meanwhile, place the sugar, spices and lemon rind and juice in a pan with the ½ pint water and heat gently until the sugar has dissolved. Bring to the boil then remove from the heat. Cool slightly, then whisk in the dissolved gelatine and cool for 20 minutes, whisking from time to time. Strain the spices and zest from the syrup in the pan and then stir in the port wine. Pour into a wetted 1½ pint mould or into stemmed glasses and chill until set.

Christmas Cake

This is a proper, fruit filled Christmas cake, but with a somewhat lighter texture.

**8 oz. butter   8 oz. soft brown sugar   4 eggs   9 oz. flour
1 level teaspoon each ground ginger, cinnamon, cloves and nutmeg
½ teaspoon salt   8 oz. sultanas   8 oz. currants
3 oz. glacé cherries, quartered and rolled in flour
5 oz. chopped mixed candied peel   2 oz. whole almonds, chopped
2 tablespoons brandy or medium sweet sherry**

Set oven to 275°F or Mark 1. Line a 7 inch square or 8 inch round cake tin. Cream together the butter and sugar in a bowl, then beat in the eggs, one at a time. Sift together the flour, spices and salt and fold into the mixture. Add the dried fruit, cherries, mixed peel and the almonds and then the brandy or sherry, a little at a time, mixing to a dropping consistency. Put the mixture into the tin, making a slight well in the centre, and bake for about 4-5 hours. Test with a skewer; when the cake is ready it will come out clean. Cover with kitchen foil if the top browns too quickly. Allow to get cold in the tin before removing. To improve the flavour, pierce the top with a skewer and feed with brandy or sherry. To ice the cake, brush all over with warmed apricot jam before applying the almond paste. Leave to dry for 2-3 days before finishing with Royal icing, as desired.

Chocolate Log Cake

This cake represents the great Yule Log burned during the Christmas festivities.

4 oz. caster sugar   **3 eggs**   **Few drops of vanilla essence**   **3 oz. flour**
½ oz. cocoa powder   **Pinch of salt**   **1 oz. butter, melted**   **2 oz. plain chocolate**
8 oz. sweetened chestnut purée   **¼ pt. double cream**   **A little sifted icing sugar**

Set oven to 375° or Mark 5. Whisk the sugar, eggs and essence together until very thick and pale in colour. Sift together the flour, cocoa powder and salt, then sift into the sugar mixture a little at a time, lightly folding in each addition. Allow the melted butter to cool slightly, then fold in. Pour the mixture into a lined and greased 7 x 11 inch Swiss Roll tin and smooth over, making sure that there is plenty into the corners. Bake for 15 to 20 minutes, or until well risen and springy to the touch. Place a piece of greaseproof paper on the table and sprinkle with caster sugar. Turn out the cake on to this, peel off the lining and trim the edges. Roll up the cake and paper together and cool on a wire rack. Break the chocolate into a bowl and melt over a basin of hot water, then fold into the chestnut purée. Whip the cream until it stands up in peaks and fold into the chocolate mixture, combining well. Unroll the cake very carefully, remove the sugared paper and spread with some of the chocolate mixture. Roll up carefully then cover with the remaining mixture, roughing up to represent bark. Chill slightly, dust with icing sugar and decorate.

Sparkling Crystallised Fruit Cake

This cake, with its lighter texture and pale fruits, makes a pleasant change.

6 oz. dried apricots   6 tablespoons whisky   8 oz. butter   8 oz. caster sugar
Grated rind and juice of 1 lemon   Grated rind and juice of 1 orange
2 oz. ground almonds   4 eggs   8 oz. flour   Pinch of salt
6 oz. multi coloured glacé cherries, coarsley chopped   4 oz. stem or crystallised ginger, chopped finely
4 oz. glacé pineapple, coarsely chopped   4 oz. candied peel, coarsely chopped
2 oz. candied mango or papaya   4 oz. walnuts, roughly chopped

Soak the apricots in the whisky for at least 4 hours. When ready, set oven to 300°F or Mark 2. Cream the butter and sugar with the lemon and orange rinds until light and fluffy, then stir in the almonds. Whisk the eggs until pale and thick, then gradually whisk into the creamed mixture until well mixed. Sift the flour and salt into the bowl and gently fold into the mixture. Stir in the orange and lemon juices, apricots, candied fruits and ginger and the walnuts. Spoon into a buttered and lined 9 inch round cake tin, and make a slight hollow in the centre. Bake for 2½ hours, then cover loosely with foil, reduce heat to 275°F or Mark 1 and bake for another 1½-2 hours until cooked through; test with a skewer, which should come out clean. Cool in the tin, then turn out and wrap in foil and store in a cool place for up to three weeks. Ice with traditional Royal icing and decorate as preferred.

Jewelled Shortbread

This rich, buttery shortbread, studded with candied fruits, makes a colourful addition to the Christmas tea table.

4 oz. butter	2 oz. multi coloured glacé cherries,
2 oz. caster sugar	washed and chopped
6 oz. flour	2 oz. flaked almonds, chopped
Pinch of salt	1 oz. angelica, chopped

Set oven to 325°F or Mark 3. Cream together the butter and sugar in a bowl until just blended, then work in the flour and salt, followed by half the cherries, almonds and angelica. Knead lightly and chill for 15 minutes. Roll out on a floured surface into a rectangle 4 inches wide and about ¼ inch thickness and cut into fingers of approximately 1 inch width. Place the fingers on to greased baking sheets and decorate with the remaining cherries, almonds and angelica. Prick the biscuit fingers with a fork lightly all over, then bake for about 20 minutes until pale gold, but do not allow to brown. Place the biscuits carefully on a wire rack to cool.

Stained Glass Window Biscuits

These delicious biscuits with their jewelled colours really catch the light when hung on the Christmas tree and are a favourite with children.

2 oz. icing sugar	**4 oz. butter**
1 tablespoon milk	**½ teaspoon vanilla essence**
6 oz. flour	**4 oz. boiled sweets in assorted colours**

Set oven to 400°F or Mark 6. Combine all the ingredients (not the boiled sweets) with the hands in a mixing bowl to form a pliable dough. Cover with cling film and chill for 45 minutes. Roll out the dough to about ⅛ inch thickness on a floured surface and cut into seasonal shapes with pastry cutters, e.g. stars, hearts, bells, etc., preferably cutting out each shape in 2 sizes. Press the smaller version of each shape on to the larger one, leaving a border of about ⅜ inch all around. This gives an attractive two dimensional effect, though not absolutely necessary. Make a hole with a skewer at the top of each biscuit for hanging, but not too near the top. Place the biscuits on baking sheets lined with non stick baking paper. Place a boiled sweet (or half each of two contrasting colours) in the middle of each biscuit, pushing the sweets right through the biscuits on to the baking paper. Bake for 7 minutes, until the sweets have melted and the biscuits are cooked. Leave to cool on the sheet. When cold, thread with ribbon or gold or silver thread and hang on the tree.

Carol Singing Pepper Cake

In Yorkshire, these spicy cakes were traditionally given to carol singers at Christmas. Cakes such as this were known as 'pepper cakes', not because they contained pepper, but because the spices were imported from the East, where lands were known collectively as the 'pepper countries'.

1½ lbs. flour	½ teaspoon ground cinnamon
8 oz. butter	1½ lbs. black treacle
8 oz. dark soft brown sugar	4 eggs, beaten
1 teaspoon ground cloves	1 teaspoon bicarbonate of soda
½ teaspoon ground ginger	4 tablespoons milk

Set oven to 325°F or Mark 3. Rub the butter into the flour in a mixing bowl until the mixture resembles fine breadcrumbs, then add the sugar and spices. Put the treacle in a small pan and heat gently until melted, but not hot or the eggs will curdle. Mix into the dry ingredients with the beaten eggs. Mix the bicarbonate of soda with the milk until dissolved and stir into the mixture, beating well. Put the mixture into a greased and lined roasting tin, about 10 inch x 14 inch, spread out evenly and bake for 1¾ hours. Cool in the tin for 15 minutes then turn out on to a wire rack to cool. Cut into slices when serving. Store in an airtight tin for a few days before eating, to allow the flavour to develop.

Crystallised Chestnuts

Sweet Chestnuts have been eaten for centuries, as soup, as a stuffing for poultry or as a sauce. In Victorian times they became popular at Christmas, either roasted or crystallised as an after dinner sweetmeat. Placed in decorative sweet cases and arranged in pretty little boxes, Crystallised Chestnuts make attractive gifts.

1 lb. fresh chestnuts	**¼ pt. water**
1 lb. granulated sugar	**A few drops of vanilla essence**

Using a sharp knife, slit the skins of the chestnuts, taking care not to cut the flesh. Place in a saucepan, cover with water and boil for 15 to 20 minutes. Drain and then, while still warm, peel off the skins. Put the granulated sugar and water into a saucepan and bring to the boil, stirring until the sugar is completely dissolved. Stir in the vanilla essence, then add the chestnuts and boil briskly for 10 to 15 minutes. Reserving the syrup, remove the chestnuts with a slotted spoon and drain on a wire rack with a dish placed underneath to catch the drips. Leave for 24 hours, then re-boil the syrup, add the chestnuts and bring back to the boil. Simmer until the chestnuts are thickly coated with the syrup, then drain as before. Allow to dry completely before packing into air-tight containers.

Turkey Broth

When the roast turkey has been eaten, it is useful to have a means of using the cold remains. This sustaining broth is ideal to come home to after a brisk post-Christmas walk.

2 oz. butter	Pinch of mixed herbs
1 onion, finely chopped	8 oz. cooked turkey, diced
1 large carrot, finely cubed	4 oz. frozen peas
8 oz. potato, cubed	4 oz. frozen runner beans, sliced
1 stick celery, chopped	½ pt. creamy milk
1 teaspoon curry powder	Parsley
1 oz. flour	Salt and pepper
1½ pts. chicken stock	Pinch of paprika to garnish

Melt the butter in a pan and add all the vegetables except the peas and beans. Stir in the curry powder and cook for a few minutes. Add the flour and gradually stir in the stock. Add the herbs, bring to the boil, cover and simmer gently for 40 minutes. Add the peas, beans and turkey meat and simmer for 15 minutes, then add the milk and parsley and season to taste. When hot, serve in bowls, sprinkling paprika on top of each bowl. Serve with hot crusty rolls.

George and Dragon

C.T.HOWARD

Wassail Punch

This drink takes its name from the Anglo Saxon toast "Waes Hael" or Good Health.

4 whole, small eating apples with 2 cloves stuck in each
8 oz. soft brown sugar   1 pt. medium sherry   1 cinnamon stick
4 pts. brown ale   Thinly pared rind of 2 oranges

Set oven to 350°F or Mark 4. Put the apples in an ovenproof dish and pour the sugar over them. Pour in the sherry, add the cinnamon stick and bake for 20 minutes, or until the apples are just beginning to soften and brown. Do not overcook. Transfer the contents into a large saucepan and pour in the brown ale with the orange rinds. Heat until it just begins to simmer; it is then ready to serve in heatproof glasses.

Sherry Cobbler

Another delightful Christmas drink.

1 measure fresh orange juice   1 measure medium sherry
Slice of orange   A little sugar   1 tablespoon port

Put the sugar into a tumbler with some crushed ice. Add the orange juice and sherry and stir. Place on top the slice of orange, with two straws through the middle. Pour the port over the orange and serve.

Lambs Wool

A hot spiced ale, popular in the Middle Ages. The name came about due to the fluffy white flesh which burst through the skins of the roasted apples which floated on top of the bowl of ale.

4 russet eating apples	**½ teaspoon ground ginger**
4 pts. ale or cider	**3 allspice berries**
6 cloves	**1 cinnamon stick, broken**
1 teaspoon grated nutmeg	**1-2 tablespoons dark soft brown sugar**

Set oven to 400°F or Mark 6. Place the apples in a baking dish with a little ale, cider or water and cook for 30 minutes until the apple flesh is 'woolly' in texture. Meanwhile heat the ale or cider, spices and sugar to taste in a large pan over a low heat until very hot, but do not allow to boil. Strain into a large serving bowl. Scoop out the apple pulp with a spoon, discarding core and pips and pile on the hot ale. Serve hot with a scoop of apple flesh in each glass; this should be eaten with a spoon.

The Bishop

A variation of mulled wine which includes port and was so called by the 19th century students of Oxford and Cambridge. It can be stored and used as desired.

6 Seville oranges	**4 oz. sugar**	**Cloves**
1½ bottles inexpensive red wine		**1 bottle ruby port**

Bake the oranges in a moderate oven for approximately 20 minutes until golden brown and then place in a large warmed bowl with 6 cloves pricked into each fruit. Add the sugar and pour in the wine, but not the port. Cover and leave in a warm place for a day. Then, squeeze the oranges into the wine and pour through a sieve. To keep for future use, bottle in sterilised bottles and seal, at this stage omitting the port. To serve, add the port to the liquid and heat in a pan, but do not boil. Serve in warmed goblets and drink hot. Or, pour into bottles and stand in a pan of simmering water; this keeps the drink hot and makes pouring easier. If Seville oranges are out of season, use 5 sweet oranges and 1 yellow grapefruit instead. However, only squeeze in half the grapefruit juice at first and then test for taste. Add the remainder if preferred.

METRIC CONVERSIONS

The weights, measures and oven temperatures used in the preceding recipes can be easily converted to their metric equivalents. The conversions listed below are only approximate, having been rounded up or down as may be appropriate.

Weights

Avoirdupois	Metric
1 oz.	just under 30 grams
4 oz. (¼ lb.)	app. 115 grams
8 oz. (½ lb.)	app. 230 grams
1 lb.	454 grams

Liquid Measures

Imperial	Metric
1 tablespoon (liquid only)	20 millilitres
1 fl. oz.	app. 30 millilitres
1 gill (¼ pt.)	app. 145 millilitres
½ pt.	app. 285 millilitres
1 pt.	app. 570 millilitres
1 qt.	app. 1.140 litres

Oven Temperatures

	°Fahrenheit	Gas Mark	°Celsius
Slow	300	2	150
	325	3	170
Moderate	350	4	180
	375	5	190
	400	6	200
Hot	425	7	220
	450	8	230
	475	9	240

Flour as specified in these recipes refers to Plain flour unless otherwise described.